The Disciple's Pocket Planner

Belonging to

_____

For the Dates

_____ to _____

New Stonemoor Academy
Manassas, Virginia

Copyright © 2022 New Stonemoor Academy.

All rights reserved.

No part of this book may be reproduced in any form or by any electronic or mechanical means, including information storage and retrieval systems, without permission in writing from the publisher, except by reviewers, who may quote brief passages in a review.

Edited by Stacy Vaka.

Scripture quotations have been taken from the Christian Standard Bible®, Copyright © 2017 by Holman Bible Publishers. Used by permission. Christian Standard Bible® and CSB® are federally registered trademarks of Holman Bible Publishers.

Printed in the United States of America.

Published by New Stonemoor Academy: PO Box 4289, Manassas, VA 20108

www.NewStonemoorAcademy.com

Contents

Goals for this Year 4
Monthly Planner 5
Vacation Days 30
Weekly Planner 31
Simple Meal Ideas 136
Chores Schedule 138
Organic Lawn Maintenance 139
Bible Study Guide 140
Sermon Listening Guide 141
Scripture to Memorize 142
Notes 143

Goals for this Year

Monthly Planner

"You are already clean because of the word I have spoken to you. Remain in me, and I in you. Just as a branch is unable to produce fruit by itself unless it remains on the vine, neither can you unless you remain in me. I am the vine; you are the branches. The one who remains in me and I in him produces much fruit, because you can do nothing without me."

— John 15:3–5

Month:

Sunday	Monday	Tuesday	Wednesday

Monthly Fruit:
Love

Year:

Thursday	Friday	Saturday	Birthdays:
☐	☐	☐	
☐	☐	☐	
☐	☐	☐	
☐	☐	☐	Reading List:
☐	☐	☐	
☐	☐	☐	

"I give you a new command: Love one another. Just as I have loved you, you are also to love one another. By this everyone will know that you are my disciples, if you love one another."
— John 13:34–35

Month:

Sunday	Monday	Tuesday	Wednesday

Monthly Fruit:
Joy

Year:

Thursday	Friday	Saturday	Birthdays:

Reading List:

"Consider it a great joy, my brothers and sisters, whenever you experience various trials, because you know that the testing of your faith produces endurance."

— James 1:2–3

Month:

Sunday	Monday	Tuesday	Wednesday

Monthly Fruit:
Peace

Year:

Thursday	Friday	Saturday	Birthdays:

Reading List:

"Do not repay anyone evil for evil. Give careful thought to do what is honorable in everyone's eyes. If possible, as far as it depends on you, live at peace with everyone."

— Romans 12:17–18

Month:

Sunday	Monday	Tuesday	Wednesday

Monthly Fruit:
Patience

Year:

Thursday	Friday	Saturday	Birthdays:
			Reading List:

"And we exhort you, brothers and sisters: warn those who are idle, comfort the discouraged, help the weak, be patient with everyone."

— 1 Thessalonians 5:14

Month:

Sunday	Monday	Tuesday	Wednesday

Monthly Fruit:
Kindness

Year:

Thursday	Friday	Saturday	Birthdays:
			Reading List:

"And be kind and compassionate to one another, forgiving one another, just as God also forgave you in Christ."
— Ephesians 4:32

Month:

Sunday	Monday	Tuesday	Wednesday

Monthly Fruit:
Goodness

Year:

Thursday	Friday	Saturday	Birthdays:
			Reading List:

"Therefore, as we have opportunity, let us work for the good of all, especially for those who belong to the household of faith."
— Galatians 6:10

Month:

Sunday	Monday	Tuesday	Wednesday

Monthly Fruit:
Endurance

Year:

Thursday	Friday	Saturday	Birthdays:

Reading List:

"And not only that, but we also boast in our afflictions, because we know that affliction produces endurance, endurance produces proven character, and proven character produces hope."
— Romans 5:3–4

Month:

Sunday	Monday	Tuesday	Wednesday

Monthly Fruit:
Gentleness

Year:

Thursday	Friday	Saturday	Birthdays:

Reading List:

"The Lord's servant must not quarrel, but must be gentle to everyone, able to teach, and patient, instructing his opponents with gentleness.

— 2 Timothy 2:24–25

Month:

Sunday	Monday	Tuesday	Wednesday

Monthly Fruit:
Faithfulness

Year:

Thursday	Friday	Saturday	Birthdays:

Reading List:

"For truly I tell you, if you have faith the size of a mustard seed, you will tell this mountain, 'Move from here to there,' and it will move. Nothing will be impossible for you."
— Matthew 17:20

Month:

Sunday	Monday	Tuesday	Wednesday

Monthly Fruit:
Humility

Year:

Thursday	Friday	Saturday	Birthdays:

Reading List:

"Do nothing out of selfish ambition or conceit, but in humility consider others as more important than yourselves."
— Philippians 2:3

Month:

Sunday	Monday	Tuesday	Wednesday

Monthly Fruit:
Self-Control

Year:

Thursday	Friday	Saturday	Birthdays:

Reading List:

"Run in such a way to win the prize. Now everyone who competes exercises self-control in everything. They do it to receive a perishable crown, but we an imperishable crown."
— 1 Corinthians 9:24–25

Month:

Sunday	Monday	Tuesday	Wednesday

Monthly Fruit:
Chastity

Year:

Thursday	Friday	Saturday	Birthdays:

Reading List:

"Therefore, brothers and sisters, in view of the mercies of God, I urge you to present your bodies as a living sacrifice, holy and pleasing to God; this is your true worship."

— Romans 12:1

Vacation Days

Weekly Planner

"Dear friends, don't overlook this one fact: With the Lord one day is like a thousand years, and a thousand years like one day. The Lord does not delay his promise, as some understand delay, but is patient with you, not wanting any to perish but all to come to repentance."

— 2 Peter 3:8–9

Month:

Day	Events	Chores	Habit Goals
Su			
M			
Tu			
W			
Th			
F			
Sa			

Weekly Promise:

"Let us make man in our image, according to our likeness. They will rule the fish of the sea, the birds of the sky, the livestock, the whole earth, and the creatures that crawl on the earth."— Genesis 1:26

| **Dinner Planner** | **Prayer Requests** |

Su

M

Tu

W

Th

F

Sa

| **Shopping List** | **Praises** |

| **To Do** | **Bible Reading** |

How I will apply this week's sermon:

Month:

Day	Events	Chores	Habit Goals

Su

M

Tu

W

Th

F

Sa

Weekly Promise:

"You will eat bread by the sweat of your brow until you return to the ground, since you were taken from it. For you are dust, and you will return to dust."— Genesis 3:19

Dinner Planner	**Prayer Requests**
Su	
M	
Tu	
W	
Th	
F	
Sa	

Shopping List	**Praises**

To Do	**Bible Reading**

How I will apply this week's sermon:

Month:

Day	Events	Chores	Habit Goals
Su			
M			
Tu			
W			
Th			
F			
Sa			

Weekly Promise:

"I will never again curse the ground because of human beings, even though the inclination of the human heart is evil from youth onward. And I will never again strike down every living thing as I have done."— Genesis 8:21

| **Dinner Planner** | **Prayer Requests** |

Su

M

Tu

W

Th

F

Sa

| **Shopping List** | **Praises** |

| **To Do** | **Bible Reading** |

How I will apply this week's sermon:

Month:

Day	Events	Chores	Habit Goals

Su

M

Tu

W

Th

F

Sa

Weekly Promise:

"Every creature that lives and moves will be food for you; as I gave the green plants, I have given you everything."
— Genesis 9:3

Dinner Planner	**Prayer Requests**
Su	
M	
Tu	
W	
Th	
F	
Sa	

Shopping List	**Praises**

To Do	**Bible Reading**

How I will apply this week's sermon:

Month:

Day	Events	Chores	Habit Goals

Su

M

Tu

W

Th

F

Sa

Weekly Promise:

"The Lord said to Abram: ...I will bless those who bless you, I will curse anyone who treats you with contempt, and all the peoples on earth will be blessed through you." — Genesis 12:1, 3

Dinner Planner	**Prayer Requests**
Su	
M	
Tu	
W	
Th	
F	
Sa	

Shopping List	**Praises**

To Do	**Bible Reading**

How I will apply this week's sermon:

Month:

Day	Events	Chores	Habit Goals

Su

M

Tu

W

Th

F

Sa

Weekly Promise:

"Your name will no longer be Abram; your name will be
Abraham, for I will make you the father of many nations."
— Genesis 17:5

| **Dinner Planner** | **Prayer Requests** |

Su

M

Tu

W

Th

F

Sa

| **Shopping List** | **Praises** |

| **To Do** | **Bible Reading** |

How I will apply this week's sermon:

Month:

Day	Events	Chores	Habit Goals

Su

M

Tu

W

Th

F

Sa

Weekly Promise:

"Now if you will carefully listen to me and keep my covenant, you will be my own possession out of all the peoples, although the whole earth is mine." — Exodus 19:5

Dinner Planner	**Prayer Requests**
Su	
M	
Tu	
W	
Th	
F	
Sa	
Shopping List	**Praises**

To Do **Bible Reading**

How I will apply this week's sermon:

Month:

Day	Events	Chores	Habit Goals

Su

M

Tu

W

Th

F

Sa

Weekly Promise:

"Know that the Lord your God is God, the faithful God who keeps his gracious covenant loyalty for a thousand generations with those who love him and keep his commands." — Deuteronomy 7:9

Dinner Planner	**Prayer Requests**
Su	
M	
Tu	
W	
Th	
F	
Sa	
Shopping List	**Praises**

To Do **Bible Reading**

How I will apply this week's sermon:

Month:

Day	Events	Chores	Habit Goals
Su			
M			
Tu			
W			
Th			
F			
Sa			

Weekly Promise:

"The hidden things belong to the Lord our God, but the revealed things belong to us and our children forever, so that we may follow all the words of this law." — Deuteronomy 29:29

| **Dinner Planner** | **Prayer Requests** |

Su

M

Tu

W

Th

F

Sa

| **Shopping List** | **Praises** |

| **To Do** | **Bible Reading** |

How I will apply this week's sermon:

Month:

Day	Events	Chores	Habit Goals

Su

M

Tu

W

Th

F

Sa

Weekly Promise:

"""Your house and kingdom will endure before me forever, and your throne will be established forever."' Nathan reported all these words and this entire vision to David." — 2 Samuel 7:16–17

Dinner Planner   **Prayer Requests**

Su

M

Tu

W

Th

F

Sa

Shopping List   **Praises**

To Do   **Bible Reading**

How I will apply this week's sermon:

Month:

Day	Events	Chores	Habit Goals

Su

M

Tu

W

Th

F

Sa

Weekly Promise:

"Do not forget the covenant that I have made with you. Do not fear other gods, but fear the Lord your God, and he will rescue you from all your enemies." — 2 Kings 17:38–39

Dinner Planner	**Prayer Requests**
Su	
M	
Tu	
W	
Th	
F	
Sa	

Shopping List   **Praises**

To Do   **Bible Reading**

How I will apply this week's sermon:

Month:

Day	Events	Chores	Habit Goals
Su			
M			
Tu			
W			
Th			
F			
Sa			

Weekly Promise:

"The surviving remnant of the house of Judah will again take root downward and bear fruit upward." — 2 Kings 19:30

Dinner Planner　　　　　　　　**Prayer Requests**

Su

M

Tu

W

Th

F

Sa

Shopping List　　　　　　　　**Praises**

To Do　　　　　　　　　　　**Bible Reading**

How I will apply this week's sermon:

Month:

Day	Events	Chores	Habit Goals
Su			
M			
Tu			
W			
Th			
F			
Sa			

Weekly Promise:

"Give thanks to the Lord, for he is good; his faithful love endures forever." — 1 Chronicles 16:34

| **Dinner Planner** | **Prayer Requests** |

Su

M

Tu

W

Th

F

Sa

Shopping List   **Praises**

To Do   **Bible Reading**

How I will apply this week's sermon:

Month:

Day	Events	Chores	Habit Goals
Su			
M			
Tu			
W			
Th			
F			
Sa			

Weekly Promise:

"I will designate a place for my people Israel and plant them, so that they may live there and not be disturbed again."
— 1 Chronicles 17:9

| **Dinner Planner** | **Prayer Requests** |

Su

M

Tu

W

Th

F

Sa

| **Shopping List** | **Praises** |

| **To Do** | **Bible Reading** |

How I will apply this week's sermon:

Month:

Day	Events	Chores	Habit Goals
Su			
M			
Tu			
W			
Th			
F			
Sa			

Weekly Promise:

"If you seek him, he will be found by you, but if you abandon him, he will reject you forever." — 1 Chronicles 28:9

Dinner Planner	**Prayer Requests**
Su	
M	
Tu	
W	
Th	
F	
Sa	

Shopping List	**Praises**

To Do	**Bible Reading**

How I will apply this week's sermon:

Month:

Day	Events	Chores	Habit Goals
Su			
M			
Tu			
W			
Th			
F			
Sa			

Weekly Promise:

"For the Lord your God is gracious and merciful; he will not turn his face away from you if you return to him."
— 2 Chronicles 30:9

Dinner Planner   **Prayer Requests**

Su

M

Tu

W

Th

F

Sa

Shopping List   **Praises**

To Do   **Bible Reading**

How I will apply this week's sermon:

Month:

Day	Events	Chores	Habit Goals
Su			
M			
Tu			
W			
Th			
F			
Sa			

Weekly Promise:

"The hand of our God is gracious to all who seek him, but his fierce anger is against all who abandon him." — Ezra 8:22

Dinner Planner	**Prayer Requests**
Su	
M	
Tu	
W	
Th	
F	
Sa	

Shopping List	**Praises**

To Do	**Bible Reading**

How I will apply this week's sermon:

Month:

Day	Events	Chores	Habit Goals

Su

M

Tu

W

Th

F

Sa

Weekly Promise:

"The Lord is a refuge for the persecuted, a refuge in times of trouble. Those who know your name trust in you because you have not abandoned those who seek you, Lord." — Psalm 9:9–10

| **Dinner Planner** | **Prayer Requests** |

Su

M

Tu

W

Th

F

Sa

| **Shopping List** | **Praises** |

| **To Do** | **Bible Reading** |

How I will apply this week's sermon:

Month:

Day	Events	Chores	Habit Goals
Su			
M			
Tu			
W			
Th			
F			
Sa			

Weekly Promise:

"For the Lord is righteous; he loves righteous deeds. The upright will see his face." — Psalm 11:7

Dinner Planner   **Prayer Requests**

Su

M

Tu

W

Th

F

Sa

Shopping List   **Praises**

To Do   **Bible Reading**

How I will apply this week's sermon:

Month:

Day	Events	Chores	Habit Goals
Su			
M			
Tu			
W			
Th			
F			
Sa			

Weekly Promise:

"Who is this person who fears the Lord? He will show him the way he should choose.... The secret counsel of the Lord is for those who fear him, and reveals his covenant to them." — Psalm 25:12, 14

Dinner Planner	**Prayer Requests**

Su

M

Tu

W

Th

F

Sa

Shopping List	**Praises**

To Do	**Bible Reading**

How I will apply this week's sermon:

Month:

Day	Events	Chores	Habit Goals
Su			
M			
Tu			
W			
Th			
F			
Sa			

Weekly Promise:

"Many pains come to the wicked, but the one who trusts in the Lord will have faithful love surrounding him." — Psalm 32:10

Dinner Planner   **Prayer Requests**

Su

M

Tu

W

Th

F

Sa

Shopping List   **Praises**

To Do   **Bible Reading**

How I will apply this week's sermon:

Month:

Day	Events	Chores	Habit Goals

Su

M

Tu

W

Th

F

Sa

Weekly Promise:

"The Lord redeems the life of his servants, and all who take refuge in him will not be punished." — Psalm 34:22

Dinner Planner	**Prayer Requests**
Su	
M	
Tu	
W	
Th	
F	
Sa	

Shopping List	**Praises**

To Do	**Bible Reading**

How I will apply this week's sermon:

Month:

Day	Events	Chores	Habit Goals

Su

M

Tu

W

Th

F

Sa

Weekly Promise:

"Trust in the Lord and do what is good; dwell in the land and live securely. Take delight in the Lord, and he will give you your heart's desires." — Psalm 37:3–4

Dinner Planner	**Prayer Requests**
Su	
M	
Tu	
W	
Th	
F	
Sa	

Shopping List	**Praises**

To Do	**Bible Reading**

How I will apply this week's sermon:

Month:

Day	Events	Chores	Habit Goals
Su			
M			
Tu			
W			
Th			
F			
Sa			

Weekly Promise:

"The Lord will protect you from all harm; he will protect your life. The Lord will protect your coming and going both now and forever." — Psalm 121:7–8

Dinner Planner **Prayer Requests**

Su

M

Tu

W

Th

F

Sa

Shopping List **Praises**

To Do **Bible Reading**

How I will apply this week's sermon:

Month:

Day	Events	Chores	Habit Goals

Su

M

Tu

W

Th

F

Sa

Weekly Promise:

"The Lord is near all who call out to him, all who call out to him with integrity. He fulfills the desires of those who fear him; he hears their cry for help and saves them." — Psalm 145:18–19

Dinner Planner	**Prayer Requests**
Su	
M	
Tu	
W	
Th	
F	
Sa	

Shopping List **Praises**

To Do **Bible Reading**

How I will apply this week's sermon:

Month:

Day	Events	Chores	Habit Goals

Su

M

Tu

W

Th

F

Sa

Weekly Promise:

"Trust in the Lord with all your heart, and do not rely on your own understanding; in all your ways know him, and he will make your paths straight." — Proverbs 3:5–6

Dinner Planner	**Prayer Requests**
Su	
M	
Tu	
W	
Th	
F	
Sa	
Shopping List	**Praises**

To Do **Bible Reading**

How I will apply this week's sermon:

Month:

Day	Events	Chores	Habit Goals
Su			
M			
Tu			
W			
Th			
F			
Sa			

Weekly Promise:

"All a person's ways seem right to him, but the Lord weighs motives. Commit your activities to the Lord, and your plans will be established." — Proverbs 16:2–3

Dinner Planner	**Prayer Requests**
Su	
M	
Tu	
W	
Th	
F	
Sa	

Shopping List	**Praises**

To Do	**Bible Reading**

How I will apply this week's sermon:

Month:

Day	Events	Chores	Habit Goals
Su			
M			
Tu			
W			
Th			
F			
Sa			

Weekly Promise:

"'Come, let's settle this,' says the Lord. 'Though your sins are scarlet, they will be as white as snow; though they are crimson red, they will be like wool.'" — Isaiah 1:18

| **Dinner Planner** | **Prayer Requests** |

Su

M

Tu

W

Th

F

Sa

| **Shopping List** | **Praises** |

| **To Do** | **Bible Reading** |

How I will apply this week's sermon:

Month:

Day	Events	Chores	Habit Goals

Su

M

Tu

W

Th

F

Sa

Weekly Promise:

"Therefore, the Lord himself will give you a sign: See, the virgin will conceive, have a son, and name him Immanuel."
— Isaiah 7:14

Dinner Planner   **Prayer Requests**

Su

M

Tu

W

Th

F

Sa

Shopping List   **Praises**

To Do   **Bible Reading**

How I will apply this week's sermon:

Month:

Day	Events	Chores	Habit Goals
Su			
M			
Tu			
W			
Th			
F			
Sa			

Weekly Promise:

"For a child will be born for us, a son will be given to us, and the government will be on his shoulders. He will be named Wonderful Counselor, Mighty God, Eternal Father, Prince of Peace." — Isaiah 9:6

Dinner Planner   **Prayer Requests**

Su

M

Tu

W

Th

F

Sa

Shopping List   **Praises**

To Do   **Bible Reading**

How I will apply this week's sermon:

Month:

Day	Events	Chores	Habit Goals

Su

M

Tu

W

Th

F

Sa

Weekly Promise:

"But those who trust in the Lord will renew their strength; they will soar on wings like eagles; they will run and not become weary, they will walk and not faint." — Isaiah 40:31

Dinner Planner	**Prayer Requests**
Su	
M	
Tu	
W	
Th	
F	
Sa	

Shopping List	**Praises**

To Do	**Bible Reading**

How I will apply this week's sermon:

Month:

Day	Events	Chores	Habit Goals
Su			
M			
Tu			
W			
Th			
F			
Sa			

Weekly Promise:

"For I will create new heavens and a new earth; the past events will not be remembered or come to mind." — Isaiah 65:17

Dinner Planner	**Prayer Requests**
Su	
M	
Tu	
W	
Th	
F	
Sa	
Shopping List	**Praises**
To Do	**Bible Reading**

How I will apply this week's sermon:

Month:

Day	Events	Chores	Habit Goals
Su			
M			
Tu			
W			
Th			
F			
Sa			

Weekly Promise:

"No longer will one teach his neighbor or his brother, saying, 'Know the Lord,' for they will all know me, from the least to the greatest of them…. For I will forgive their iniquity and never again remember their sin." — Jeremiah 31:34

Dinner Planner   **Prayer Requests**

Su

M

Tu

W

Th

F

Sa

Shopping List   **Praises**

To Do   **Bible Reading**

How I will apply this week's sermon:

Month:

Day	Events	Chores	Habit Goals

Su

M

Tu

W

Th

F

Sa

Weekly Promise:

"In the days of those kings, the God of the heavens will set up a kingdom that will never be destroyed.... It will crush all those kingdoms and bring them to an end, but will itself endure forever." — Daniel 2:44

Dinner Planner **Prayer Requests**

Su

M

Tu

W

Th

F

Sa

Shopping List **Praises**

To Do **Bible Reading**

How I will apply this week's sermon:

Month:

Day	Events	Chores	Habit Goals
Su			
M			
Tu			
W			
Th			
F			
Sa			

Weekly Promise:

"In that day I will restore the fallen shelter of David: I will repair its gaps, restore its ruins, and rebuild it as the days of old."
— Amos 9:11

| **Dinner Planner** | **Prayer Requests** |

Su

M

Tu

W

Th

F

Sa

| **Shopping List** | **Praises** |

| **To Do** | **Bible Reading** |

How I will apply this week's sermon:

Month:

Day	Events	Chores	Habit Goals

Su

M

Tu

W

Th

F

Sa

Weekly Promise:

"They will beat their swords into plows and their spears into pruning knives. Nation will not take up the sword against nation, and they will never again train for war." — Micah 4:3

Dinner Planner	**Prayer Requests**
Su	
M	
Tu	
W	
Th	
F	
Sa	

Shopping List	**Praises**

To Do	**Bible Reading**

How I will apply this week's sermon:

Month:

Day	Events	Chores	Habit Goals

Su

M

Tu

W

Th

F

Sa

Weekly Promise:

"Bethlehem Ephrathah, you are small among the clans of Judah; one will come from you to be ruler over Israel for me. His origin is from antiquity, from ancient times." — Micah 5:2

Dinner Planner	**Prayer Requests**
Su	
M	
Tu	
W	
Th	
F	
Sa	

Shopping List	**Praises**

To Do	**Bible Reading**

How I will apply this week's sermon:

Month:

Day	Events	Chores	Habit Goals

Su

M

Tu

W

Th

F

Sa

Weekly Promise:
"Shout in triumph, Daughter Jerusalem! Look, your King is coming to you; he is righteous and victorious, humble and riding on a donkey, on a colt, the foal of a donkey." — Zechariah 9:9

| **Dinner Planner** | **Prayer Requests** |

Su

M

Tu

W

Th

F

Sa

| **Shopping List** | **Praises** |

| **To Do** | **Bible Reading** |

How I will apply this week's sermon:

Month:

Day	Events	Chores	Habit Goals
Su			
M			
Tu			
W			
Th			
F			
Sa			

Weekly Promise:

"My name will be great among the nations, from the rising of the sun to its setting. Incense and pure offerings will be presented in my name in every place because my name will be great among the nations." — Malachi 1:11

Dinner Planner	**Prayer Requests**
Su	
M	
Tu	
W	
Th	
F	
Sa	

Shopping List	**Praises**

To Do	**Bible Reading**

How I will apply this week's sermon:

Month:

Day	Events	Chores	Habit Goals

Su

M

Tu

W

Th

F

Sa

Weekly Promise:

"Come to me, all of you who are weary and burdened, and I will give you rest.... For my yoke is easy and my burden is light."
— Matthew 11:28, 30

Dinner Planner	**Prayer Requests**
Su	
M	
Tu	
W	
Th	
F	
Sa	

Shopping List	**Praises**

To Do	**Bible Reading**

How I will apply this week's sermon:

Month:

Day	Events	Chores	Habit Goals

Su

M

Tu

W

Th

F

Sa

Weekly Promise:

"I am the resurrection and the life. The one who believes in me, even if he dies, will live. Everyone who lives and believes in me will never die." — John 11:25–26

Dinner Planner	**Prayer Requests**
Su	
M	
Tu	
W	
Th	
F	
Sa	

Shopping List	**Praises**

To Do	**Bible Reading**

How I will apply this week's sermon:

Month:

Day	Events	Chores	Habit Goals
Su			
M			
Tu			
W			
Th			
F			
Sa			

Weekly Promise:

"For all have sinned and fall short of the glory of God; they are justified freely by his grace through the redemption that is in Christ Jesus." — Romans 3:23–24

| **Dinner Planner** | **Prayer Requests** |

Su

M

Tu

W

Th

F

Sa

| **Shopping List** | **Praises** |

| **To Do** | **Bible Reading** |

How I will apply this week's sermon:

Month:

Day	Events	Chores	Habit Goals

Su

M

Tu

W

Th

F

Sa

Weekly Promise:

"For since death came through a man, the resurrection of the dead also comes through a man. For just as in Adam all die, so also in Christ all will be made alive." — 1 Corinthians 15:21–22

Dinner Planner	**Prayer Requests**
Su	
M	
Tu	
W	
Th	
F	
Sa	
Shopping List	**Praises**

To Do **Bible Reading**

How I will apply this week's sermon:

Month:

Day	Events	Chores	Habit Goals

Su

M

Tu

W

Th

F

Sa

Weekly Promise:

"There is no Jew or Greek, slave or free, male and female; since you are all one in Christ Jesus. And if you belong to Christ, then you are Abraham's seed, heirs according to the promise." — Galatians 3:28–29

Dinner Planner	**Prayer Requests**
Su	
M	
Tu	
W	
Th	
F	
Sa	

Shopping List **Praises**

To Do **Bible Reading**

How I will apply this week's sermon:

Month:

Day	Events	Chores	Habit Goals
Su			
M			
Tu			
W			
Th			
F			
Sa			

Weekly Promise:

"You know those who taught you, and you know that from infancy you have known the sacred Scriptures, which are able to give you wisdom for salvation through faith in Christ Jesus." — 2 Timothy 3:14–15

Dinner Planner   **Prayer Requests**

Su

M

Tu

W

Th

F

Sa

Shopping List   **Praises**

To Do   **Bible Reading**

How I will apply this week's sermon:

Month:

Day	Events	Chores	Habit Goals
Su			
M			
Tu			
W			
Th			
F			
Sa			

Weekly Promise:

"You are being guarded by God's power through faith for a salvation that is ready to be revealed in the last time."
— 1 Peter 1:5

| **Dinner Planner** | **Prayer Requests** |

Su

M

Tu

W

Th

F

Sa

| **Shopping List** | **Praises** |

| **To Do** | **Bible Reading** |

How I will apply this week's sermon:

Month:

Day	Events	Chores	Habit Goals

Su

M

Tu

W

Th

F

Sa

Weekly Promise:

"If we confess our sins, he is faithful and righteous to forgive us our sins and to cleanse us from all unrighteousness."
— 1 John 1:9

Dinner Planner	**Prayer Requests**
Su	
M	
Tu	
W	
Th	
F	
Sa	
Shopping List	**Praises**
To Do	**Bible Reading**

How I will apply this week's sermon:

Month:

Day	Events	Chores	Habit Goals
Su			
M			
Tu			
W			
Th			
F			
Sa			

Weekly Promise:

"And the world with its lust is passing away, but the one who does the will of God remains forever." — 1 John 2:17

Dinner Planner   **Prayer Requests**

Su

M

Tu

W

Th

F

Sa

Shopping List   **Praises**

To Do   **Bible Reading**

How I will apply this week's sermon:

Month:

Day	Events	Chores	Habit Goals
Su			
M			
Tu			
W			
Th			
F			
Sa			

Weekly Promise:

"If we ask anything according to his will, he hears us. And if we know that he hears whatever we ask, we know that we have what we have asked of him." — 1 John 5:14–15

Dinner Planner   **Prayer Requests**

Su

M

Tu

W

Th

F

Sa

Shopping List   **Praises**

To Do   **Bible Reading**

How I will apply this week's sermon:

Month:

Day	Events	Chores	Habit Goals
Su			
M			
Tu			
W			
Th			
F			
Sa			

Weekly Promise:

"See! I stand at the door and knock. If anyone hears my voice and opens the door, I will come in to him and eat with him, and he with me." — Revelation 3:20

Dinner Planner	**Prayer Requests**
Su	
M	
Tu	
W	
Th	
F	
Sa	

Shopping List	**Praises**

To Do	**Bible Reading**

How I will apply this week's sermon:

Month:

Day	Events	Chores	Habit Goals

Su

M

Tu

W

Th

F

Sa

Weekly Promise:

"He will wipe away every tear from their eyes. Death will be no more; grief, crying, and pain will be no more, because the previous things have passed away." — Revelation 21:4

| **Dinner Planner** | **Prayer Requests** |

Su

M

Tu

W

Th

F

Sa

| **Shopping List** | **Praises** |

| **To Do** | **Bible Reading** |

How I will apply this week's sermon:

Month:

Day	Events	Chores	Habit Goals
Su			
M			
Tu			
W			
Th			
F			
Sa			

Weekly Promise:

"Look, I am coming soon! Blessed is the one who keeps the words of the prophecy of this book." — Revelation 22:7

| **Dinner Planner** | **Prayer Requests** |

Su

M

Tu

W

Th

F

Sa

| **Shopping List** | **Praises** |

| **To Do** | **Bible Reading** |

How I will apply this week's sermon:

Simple Meal Ideas

Dinners

1. Pot roast
2. Vegetable noodle soup
3. Shepherd's pie
4. Beans and rice
5. Stuffed squash/peppers
6. Pasta with vegetables
7. Pulled meat sandwiches
8. French onion soup
9. Noodle casserole
10. Risotto
11. Steak
12. Loaded baked potatoes
13. Shish kabobs
14. Ramen/lo mein
15. Stew
16. Macaroni and cheese
17. Hamburgers/hot dogs
18. Grilled cheese
19. Hash
20. Baked ziti/lasagna
21. Fish fry
22. Pizza
23. Jambalaya
24. Burritos
25. Tacos
26. Quesadillas
27. Chili
28. Nachos
29. Stir fry
30. Fried rice

Lunches

1. Sandwiches
2. Salad
3. Tortilla wraps
4. Chips and salsa/dip
5. Stuffed pitas
6. Hummus and dippers
7. Charcuterie board
8. Leftovers

Breakfasts

1. Eggs/omelets and meat
2. Muffins/quick bread
3. Meat and potatoes
4. Oatmeal
5. Biscuits & sausage gravy
6. Pancakes/waffles
7. Toast with spread
8. Yogurt

Road Trip Foods

- **Breakfasts:** Granola bars, muffins, fruit
- **Lunches:** Sandwiches, crackers, cheese
- **Dinners:** Cold chicken or shredded meat, chips, raw vegetables
- **Snacks:** Cookies, beef jerky, pretzels

Camping Foods

- **Breakfasts:** Sausage, pie iron breakfast sandwiches, campfire toast
- **Lunches:** Sandwiches, charcuterie, pie iron grilled cheese
- **Dinners:** Hot dogs/brats, pie iron pizza, shish kabobs
- **Snacks:** Trail mix, s'mores, campfire popcorn

Party Courses

- Bread
- Appetizer
- Soup and/or salad
- Main course
- Side dishes
- Dessert
- Beverages

Chores Schedule

Every Day
- Laundry
- Put things away
- _____

Every Week
- Clean toilets, sinks, and tubs
- Wipe windows and mirrors
- Vacuum and mop
-
- _____

Every Month
1st Week: Kitchen and Dining Room
- Clean refrigerator and oven
- Wipe backsplash and baseboards
- Kitchen and dining room laundry
- _____

2nd Week: Living and Family Rooms
- Dust and wipe baseboards
- Vacuum and/or wipe couches
- Living and family room laundry
- _____

3rd Week: Bedrooms
- Dust and wipe baseboards
- Wash bedding
- Flip and rotate mattresses
- _____

4th Week: Bathrooms
- Scrub grout
- Bathroom laundry
- Organize cabinets
- _____

5th Week (occasional): Annual Tasks
- Organize hall closets and utility room
- Shampoo carpets
- Wash curtains
- Clean garage
- Power wash house exterior
- _____

Organic Lawn Maintenance

January
- Prune trees & shrubs
- Put Christmas away
- _____

February
- Start indoor seeds
- _____

March
- Add compost to garden
- Clean gutters
- Copper on fruit treats
- Decorate for Easter
- Mow & weed weekly
- Prepare garden beds
- Sweep chimney
- _____
- _____

April
- Divide perennials
- Mow & weed weekly
- Prune flowering trees
- Put Easter décor away
- Thuricide on garden
- Transplant seedlings
- Weekly clay on fruit trees
- _____
- _____

May
- Deadhead flowers
- Mow & weed weekly
- Plant other garden plants
- Thuricide on garden
- Two weekly sulfur treatments on fruit plants
- Weekly clay on fruit trees
- _____
- _____

June
- Deadhead flowers
- Horticulture oil on roses
- Mow & weed weekly
- Thin/prune fruit trees
- Weekly clay on fruit trees
- _____
- _____

July
- Deadhead flowers
- Horticulture oil on roses
- Mow & weed weekly
- Thin/prune fruit trees
- Weekly clay on fruit trees
- _____
- _____

August
- Deadhead flowers
- Horticulture oil on roses
- Mow & weed weekly
- Thin/prune fruit trees
- Weekly clay on fruit trees
- _____
- _____

September
- Biweekly clay on fruit trees
- Clean gutters
- Clean up garden beds
- Deadhead flowers
- Divide perennials
- Mow & weed weekly
- _____
- _____

October
- Apply mulch to garden
- Deadhead flowers
- Harvest remaining fruit
- Mow & weed weekly
- _____
- _____

November
- Copper on fruit trees
- Prune shrubs
- Turn off outside water
- _____

December
- Christmas décor
- _____

Bible Study Guide

Suggestions for Notetaking

- Highlight any phrases that are repeated.
- Number any lists that are found.
- Draw an illustration or doodle of any comparisons that are made.
- Put a check mark next to commands given.

Discussion Questions

1. How are you already living today's message?
2. How can you improve on living the message?
3. What did the passage say about God?
4. What did the passage say about the world?
5. What did the passage say about you?
6. What past experiences have you had that relate to this passage?

Prayer Prompts

1. How did the passage awe you about God?
2. What did the passage say about God's will?
3. What needs did the passage bring to light?
4. What sins did the passage bring to light that you need to be forgiven for?
5. What kinds of temptations is this passage warning us about?
6. How did the passage inspire you to honor God this week?

Sermon Listening Guide

Investigate

- WHO are the people mentioned in the sermon?
- WHAT is the main point of the sermon?
- WHEN do the events in the sermon take place?
- WHERE do the events in the sermon take place?
- WHY is the message of the sermon important?
- HOW should you apply the message of the sermon this week?

Dig Deeper

- What are some new terms to define?
- Is there any extra information in your Bible's notes and/or footnotes?
- What about the sermon would you like to discuss with your family and/or friends?

Takeaways

- What are some things the pastor or speaker said that you thought were interesting?
- What are some things you will pray for this week?

Scripture to Memorize

Notes

Page	Topic

If found, please return to:

www.ingramcontent.com/pod-product-compliance
Lightning Source LLC
Chambersburg PA
CBHW020852160426
43192CB00007B/889